Someone is sick-

How do I say Goodbye?

Jill A. Johnson-Young, LCSW

Published by Central Counseling Services
6940 Indiana Ave, Suite 275
Riverside CA 92506

www.yourpaththroughgrief.com

Copyright February 2018
Library of Congress Control Number: 2018904737
ISBN: 978-0-9997886-1-5

This book was written for all the children I've worked with in hospice who were facing the loss of someone they loved, the children I see in my practice who are coping with a loved one dying, and the children of families in my dementia group who watch their loved ones fading away.

Saying goodbye is never easy- but having permission to cope in a way that fits the child and understanding what's happening can make a tremendous difference. Being prepared can lighten the impact of grief and remembering people we love who have died keeps them with us and makes them part of us. I hope this will reach children and families who are trying to find their path to their own goodbyes.

May you find your own peace and keep their memories with you.

Jill

Someone you love is sick. The doctor says they will not get better.

Sometimes even medicine and hospitals, doctors and nurses, can't fix some kinds of sickness.

That may be confusing.

2

When you get sick your family gives you medicine and may take you to the doctor. You expect to get better- and you do!

But sometimes, no matter how hard they try, doctors can't make a disease stop. The person you know may still go to the doctor's office sometimes. But those visits are not to make them get well. The doctors are trying to make them not feel so bad.

5

Not feeling so bad, or even feeling better because there is less pain is not the same as getting well. (No matter how much you wish it!)

7

8

When you visit, their room may look like a hospital, even at home. There may be a lot of medicines, a hospital bed that can move, oxygen tanks or a machine that makes oxygen, and there may be plastic tubes to carry oxygen to their nose. Those things all make them more comfortable.

The good news is, you can probably still climb in bed to snuggle with them, and tubes won't hurt you or them. Just ask an adult to help you.

11

12

When someone is so sick that they can't get better we eventually have to get ready, because they are now terminally ill, which means they are going to die.

You need to know that they did not choose to be so sick, and they do not want to leave you. Their body just can't fight anymore. You can ask any of the adults around you any questions you have. You may want to know more – and that's okay.

15

How do we say goodbye?

There are no rules. You get to say it the way you want to, or not at all if you just can't.

17

You probably have a lot of feelings happening- you may be sad, or feel empty, or be mad. Or maybe you are feeling something else? It's normal to feel like you are mixed up about it all when someone is going to die. Sometimes emojis help us name or describe our feelings.

19

20

When we think about them dying, and not being here with us, it can help to remember the things you learned from them, and what's special about them. Did they teach you something important? Or did you have a special day or thing you did together?

Talking about the things you will never forget may help them know just how much you love them and will miss them. It may help you get ready, too, because remembering those special things about them will stay with you.

23

If they can't talk anymore, which can happen when someone is dying, you might write them a letter or draw a picture of the two of you. You can leave it with them or save it. Looking at it later may help you when you are missing them.

25

You can also just sit with them and hold their hand. Even if they can't talk, or if they are asleep – they can hear you. They will know you are there.

You won't hurt them and hearing your voice might make them feel happy and safe.

27

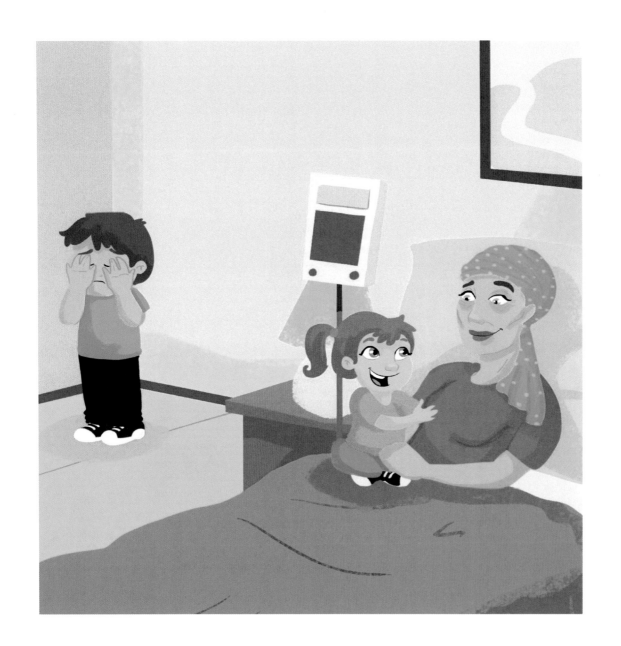

28

You can cry, or smile, or even laugh.

Or maybe even all of those!

After they die, you will always remember them, why they mattered to you...

How much you still love them...and that their love will always be with you.

31

32

Some things for the big people reading this:

Preparing for a death in a child's life:

- Be *honest* about what is occurring

- Explain the dying process at an age appropriate level if they will be present for any part of it, and what will happen afterward. *Kids do better with information.*

- Children need to know that death is a normal and expected part of life. Treating it that way they will teach healthy coping skills and make them more adept at coping with death as adults.

- If kiddos are helped to say goodbye, and to remember their loved one as they were- not perfect, but for what was special about them- they will learn a valuable lesson for the rest of their life.

- If you are going to be busy or emotionally distracted and your child is going to be with you with the terminally ill loved one: consider asking another adult who is more emotionally available to keep an eye on your child in that moment. It really is hard to take care of a dying person, a child, and yourself all at the same time.

- If you have a belief system about an afterlife, now is the time to share it, but not to expect them to share it completely. They will eventually use this experience to help shape their own beliefs.

Do not ever insist that a child touch or kiss someone who is dying or has died.

Some tips for helping children with their grief

- Include kids if they want to be part of funeral or memorial services. Give them permission to change their minds- even during the service.

- Please be cautious about telling children that their loved one was needed more in the afterlife than here, with your child. Kiddos are very concrete thinkers. If they are told a higher power had a plan to take their loved one away it can cause fear and anger, not a feeling of support.

- Use realistic words. If you tell a child that a loved one went to "go to sleep" they may not sleep at bedtime for a *long* time!

- If they have had other losses, a new one will bring them back. Losses include pets, people, moving, divorces-everything.

- Be cautious about how you describe seeing a loved one again after they have died. Children sometimes interpret that to mean if they die sooner they will be with their loved one sooner. Their thinking is concrete.

- Shield them from comments about needing to be strong or taking care of other family members. They are, after all, children. They do not need to feel that they are supposed to be responsible for anyone else when they are trying to grieve the death of someone they loved. Remember, being strong usually implies not showing emotions.

- Don't insist that a child approach a casket. Many adults can't cope with that. Be supportive, give permission, but do not make them do something that is scary for them.

• You can suggest that your child write a note or draw a picture you can tuck into the casket if they have a need to do something, but again, do not insist.

• Locate a safe space that is quiet for your child at any services being held if they need to get away from the emotions or the people. Those experiences are overwhelming for adults sometimes, and receiving lines are simply a lot of hands to touch and people to listen to. That's adult space.

• Say the loved one's name, talk about them after the funeral and remember them on special days.

• Let them cry when they need to, but remember they can laugh and smile, too.

• Remember that we all grieve differently, and at different speeds. Even kiddos.

• Reassure them that the people they count on are not sick, are not dying, and that their world is still secure. Tell them what will happen if their primary caregivers die- that's a huge fear for little people who have become aware of the reality of death.

- Keep in mind that while your grief may take time, children operate differently because of their brain development. Your child may appear to recover more quickly. That's not because the loss matters less to them. It means they are being children.

- Children often see their loved ones come back and visit. That's normal. They also see their loved one growing up with them, and will include them in their special days, holidays, and other events. That's normal. It means they are keeping their memory and place in their life. It should be encouraged.

About the author:

Jill Johnson-Young, LCSW, is a certified Grief Recovery Facilitator, Co-Founder of a successful group therapy practice in Riverside, California, and a therapist specializing in grief and loss, trauma, and children and families. She has decades of experience with hospice, where she specialized in pediatric care and provided children's grief groups in local schools. Jill trains therapists and social workers in areas that include correctly treating childhood trauma, grief and loss, and dementia care. She holds a BA from UC Riverside, and her MSW from the University of South Florida. Jill is the creator of Your Path Through Grief, which is a year-long, comprehensive one of a kind, grief support program. She is also the author "Your own path through grief workbook" and the soon to be published book "Don't Grieve like that! How to grieve your way from a rebellious widow." Jill is active in the dementia community, and facilitates a support group in her area.

Made in the USA
Monee, IL
06 June 2021